How Puerto Ricans Made the US Mainland Home

How Puerto Ricans Made the US Mainland Home

LOURDES DÁVILA

rosen
central®

New York

To my mother, Altagracia del Valle de Dávila, and my daughter, Beatriz Juana Dávila Stewart

Published in 2019 by the Rosen Publishing Group, Inc.
29 East 21st Street, New York, NY 10010

Copyright 2019 by The Rosen Publishing Group, Inc.
First Edition

Cataloging-in-Publication Data

Names: Dávila, Lourdes, author.
Title: How Puerto Ricans made the US mainland home / Lourdes Dávila.
Description: New York : Rosen Central, 2019. | Series: Coming to America: the history of immigration to the United States | Includes glossary and index. | Audience: Grades 5–8.
Identifiers: ISBN 9781508181354 (library bound) | ISBN 9781508181361 (pbk.)
Subjects: LCSH: Puerto Ricans—United States—Juvenile literature. | Immigrants—United States—History—Juvenile literature. | United States—Emigration and immigration—History—Juvenile literature.
Classification: LCC F1958.3 D385 2019 | DDC 973'.04687295—dc23

Manufactured in the United States of America

CONTENTS

Introduction

Members of the Puerto Rican community in Kissimmee, Florida, gather in a bakery on July 25, 2015. In recent years, many Puerto Ricans coming to the mainland United States have settled in Florida.

On a Wednesday morning, September 20, 2017, Hurricane Maria made landfall on the island of Puerto Rico as a category 4 storm. The storm wreaked havoc on the island's already weakened energy infrastructure, leaving Puerto Rico in the dark and without water. As this Caribbean island and US territory struggled to overcome the catastrophe and humanitarian crisis that ensued, Puerto Ricans living in the mainland United States moved into action, working alone and in groups to provide assistance, lead relief efforts, and impress upon non–Puerto Rican Americans and the world that help was badly needed.

Stateside Puerto Ricans, from factory workers to artists to doctors and professors, were desperate for news of their loved ones and took to the internet, setting up dedicated sites to communicate information and gather supplies and money.

Long after the hurricane, those sites continued to operate as a network that tied together mainland Puerto Ricans with their families and friends on the island. Many organized relief efforts. Many worked to get their family members off the island and onto the mainland.

On September 30, the websites Latino Rebels and Common Dreams both published "The Cruelest Storm: A Statement for Puerto Rico." Spearheaded by Aurea María Sotomayor-Miletti, a Puerto Rican poet and professor at the University of Pittsburgh, the letter denounced Puerto Rico's colonial status and called on US politicians to repeal permanently both the Merchant Marine Act of 1920, which forbids non-US ships from carrying goods to Puerto Rico, and the Puerto Rico Oversight, Management, and Economic Stability Act (PROMESA), a law passed in 2016 to pay off Puerto Rico's debt, which has made Puerto Rico's economic recovery nearly impossible. The statement was cosigned by more than two hundred intellectuals, many of them Puerto Rican academics, both stateside and living on the island.

On October 1, María del Rosario Dávila, a Puerto Rican computer programmer from Stow, Massachusetts, flew to Miami International Airport to pick up her ninety-year-old mother, Altagracia del Valle, a Puerto Rican lawyer with a master's in chemistry from Fordham University. As she waited at the gate for American Airlines flight 1299 to arrive from San Juan, Dávila was told by airport staff that the previous flight had engaged eighty wheelchairs to assist the elderly and infirm fleeing the island. The flight her mother was on would require thirty-seven more. It took the concerted effort of Dávila and her five siblings (three who live stateside and two who live on the island) to get their mother to the mainland and away from a home without electricity, water, or phone services.

On that same day, Bobby Sanabria, a Puerto Rican musician, filmmaker, and educator born and raised in the South Bronx, New York, shared a quote by fellow Bronx-born-and-raised Puerto Rican associate Supreme Court justice Sonia Sotomayor on his Facebook page. Sotomayor's words reaffirmed her bonds with the island and underscored the spirit of perseverance of the Puerto Rican people.

On October 6, Atlantic Records released "It's Almost Like Praying," a song conceived by Bronx-raised Puerto Rican composer and playwright Lin-Manuel Miranda. The creator of the award-winning Broadway productions *In the Heights* and *Hamilton* curated a roster of famous Puerto Ricans, including Marc Anthony, Jennifer Lopez, Pedro Capó, Rita Moreno, PJ sin Suela, Ednita Nazario, and Luis Fonsi, who joined forces to record the song derived from the well-known "Maria" of *West Side Story*, the 1957 Broadway musical (adapted to film in 1961) that fictionalized the gang wars among Puerto Ricans and other groups in 1950s New York. All proceeds from the song were destined to assist the Puerto Rico relief efforts.

By November 30, 208,000 people from Puerto Rico had landed at airports in Florida since the hurricane, and 7,756 Puerto Rican students had enrolled in public schools across that state. It was already clear that this migration to the mainland would be larger than any other in Puerto Rican history. A November 2017 NBC News article quoted University of Central Florida history professor Luis Martínez-Fernández, who said, "Puerto Rico will be seen by historians as before and after Maria." Martínez-Fernández estimated that between 500,000 and 750,000 Puerto Ricans would leave the island within the first five years after the hurricane.

Not all Puerto Ricans who have migrated to Florida or other states will remain permanently on the mainland and make it their new home; many, especially the elderly population, returned to the island within a few months. More will return over time after services are fully restored in their communities or when they can find ways of continuing their lives on the island. Many, though, will stay, supported by a strong and thriving Puerto Rican community in the United States. They have and will continue to contribute to and shape the changing social, cultural, political, and economic landscape of their adopted home.

COMINGS AND GOINGS

The latest episode of Puerto Rican migration to the mainland United States, with its movement to and from the island, is by no means a novel and unusual event. Such a back-and-forth migration pattern is made possible because, as we shall see, unlike individuals from other countries who seek to enter the United States to forge new lives, Puerto Ricans, since 1917, are born citizens of the United States. As such, they do not suffer the consequences of US immigration laws that immigrants from foreign nations do. Puerto Ricans may move freely from the island to the mainland, and many of them have done so with a great deal of frequency. One could argue then, as author

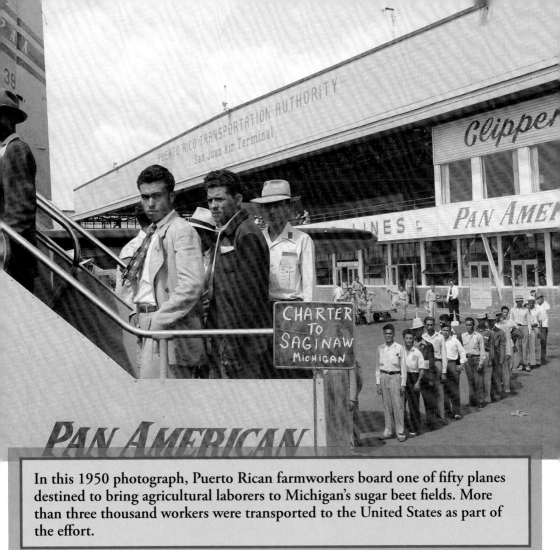

In this 1950 photograph, Puerto Rican farmworkers board one of fifty planes destined to bring agricultural laborers to Michigan's sugar beet fields. More than three thousand workers were transported to the United States as part of the effort.

Hugo Rodríguez Vecchini did in his foreword to the 1994 anthology *The Commuter Nation: Perspectives on Puerto Rican Migration*, that the physical limits of Puerto Rico do not lie in the geographical limits of the Caribbean island. Rather, they extend to every state where Puerto Ricans have made their new homes.

The migration of Puerto Ricans to the United States has always been marked by the desired certainty of a possible return. At the start of the twentieth century, when the voyage was done by water in the SS *Borinquen*, the SS *Coamo*, and other liners, as described by tobacco worker Bernardo Vega in his memoirs, the possibility of a return was deemed much harder. At that time, as was the case for so many immigrants, a move to the United States was almost certainly permanent.

Later on, however, air travel closed the distance between the island and the states. As a result, the definition of the Puerto Rican nation, as author Luis Rafael Sánchez immortalized in his 1984 essay "The Flying Bus" ("La guagua aérea"), would be defined by a continuous airborne migration that would put national identity "in the air." Some Puerto Ricans have migrated to the United States with the intention to stay but then return to the island. Others have migrated to the United States with full intentions of returning but often stay. They have a limitless ability to move back and forth, unhindered by time, space, or immigration law. Therefore, when discussing the migration of Puerto Ricans to the mainland, there are two dimensions implicit within the term "migration" that should be discussed. One is the human dimension, that is "migration" as the movement of people from one place to another, usually with the intention of settling in a new location. However, the term "migration" also calls to mind a zoological dimension, that is, the back-and-forth movement of animals across territories as the seasons change.

The large wave of Puerto Rican migration to the mainland as a result of Hurricane Maria made visible to the entire world just how large, complex, layered, and rich the Puerto Rican presence in the United States is, how unique its status, and how varied and accomplished its population. We can see the Caribbean island and its people as covering a mere 100 miles (160 kilometers) by 33 miles (53 km) of territory in the Antilles or we can understand it as a land and a people that have extended their boundaries throughout the continental United States. No matter how one interprets Puerto Rican history or what opinions one holds about it, the undeniable fact, as laid out in *West Side Story*, is that "Puerto Rico is in America!"

From Borikén to Puerto Rico

When did the Caribbean island of Puerto Rico acquire its current name? And when and how was the Puerto Rican identity formed? Puerto Ricans today, both on the island and the mainland, share indigenous Taino, Spanish, and African blood and cultural traits in multiple and varied ways.

This section of a sixteenth-century map of the Caribbean Sea shows Puerto Rico and its neighboring islands with geographic place names in Latin.

THE BIRTH OF A NAME

On November 19, 1493, the European explorer Christopher Columbus arrived at the island of Borikén (an indigenous Taino word meaning "Great land of the valiant and noble lord") and claimed it for Spain. However, at that time, the island was hardly up for grabs. In fact, it was already populated by the indigenous Tainos, members of the Arawakan people. Columbus gave the island the name San Juan Bautista (or St. John the Baptist, in English), and its main port was named

Juan Ponce de León was the first colonial governor of Puerto Rico.

VISA   UNITED STAT
OF AMERIC

Puerto Rico. With the movement of merchants through the port, fairly soon the island and the port exchanged names, and the island became known as Puerto Rico while the main city kept the name San Juan.

Historians believe that the Spanish explorer and conquistador Juan Ponce de León traveled with Christopher Columbus on the latter's second voyage, when Columbus landed in Puerto Rico. Ponce de León first explored the island as early as 1506. He was well received by the indigenous population, as he promised to assist them in their conflict with the Carib Indians, whom they feared. King Ferdinand II of Aragon appointed Juan Ponce de León as the first governor of the island in 1509. Although he had found gold in his first voyage to the island and initially even planned to have a foundry, he soon discovered that the island's riches were in sugar and developed the sugar plantation system.

The Spaniards on the island controlled and made use of the indigenous population by means of the encomienda system. Under this system, the Spanish crown assigned a number of members of the native population to the Spaniards settling the island. The encomienda system was a form of slavery, and extreme working conditions, poor treatment, and illness led to the death of almost the entirety of the Taino population. As a result, the Spanish crown allowed the importation of African enslaved people to the island. According to scholar María E. Pérez y González in her book, *The New Americans: Puerto Ricans in the United States*, there were about sixty thousand African enslaved people on the southern coast of Puerto Rico at the height of production in the sugar plantations, between 1825 and 1845.

From its food to its religion to its music, the culture of Puerto Rico is syncretic. Just like its people, who are the result of a combination of Spanish, African, and Taino blood, Puerto Ricans are mostly Catholic but with strong traces of African and Taino spiritual practices and symbols. This blend of cultural and religious traditions is visible, for instance, in the

A group of Puerto Rican women wear traditional dresses during a celebration at Kingdom of God Church in Orlando, Florida, on October 4, 2016.

celebration of Roman Catholic saints' feast days with *vejigante* costumes—representative of a traditional masked trickster character from African culture—and other elements of Santeria tradition.

In addition to religious practices, the unique cultural blend of Puerto Rico can be heard in its dialect of Spanish, which contains many elements from the indigenous Taino Arawakan language. Furthermore, Puerto Rican music is equally syncretic, mixing the sounds and rhythms of the classical Spanish and European guitar or violin with Taino instruments, such as the maraca, and African conga drums.

The social hierarchy in colonial Puerto Rico was largely fixed, placing the migrant Spanish from Europe above criollos (those born in the New World of Spanish descent) and enslaved people. Nonetheless, miscegenation—the mixing of races through marriage or otherwise—led to a very complex racial social fabric. In 2005, the American Journal of Physical Anthropology published the results of a DNA study overseen by Juan Martínez-Cruzado, a molecular biologist at the University of Puerto Rico at Mayagüez. The study showed that the DNA of a representative sample of Puerto Rican subjects revealed "maternal ancestries...of 61.3% Amerindian, 27.2% sub-Saharan African, and 11.5% West Eurasian."

This engraving of an eighteenth-century drawing by Luis Paret y Alcázar depicts a Puerto Rican enslaved woman carrying a young child. It is one of many drawings published in *Collection of Spanish Costumes* (1777), by Juan de la Cruz Cano y Olmedilla.

A "FOUR-STOREYED" IDENTITY

In his essay "Puerto Rico: The Four-Storeyed Country," Puerto Rican essayist José Luis González explains the development of Puerto Rican identity and nationalism using the metaphor of a building with four stories. The period from the conquest to the end of the nineteenth century contains the first two "floors." The first floor covers the period from 1515 to 1815, and it lays the groundwork for Puerto Rican identity. It is characterized by the development and rise of a popular culture heavily influenced by Afro-Antillean roots and the contributions of the black and mixed-race population. There is no true Puerto Rican identity without the culture of the island's colonial enslaved population.

González dates the second floor from roughly 1815 to 1898. In 1815, Spain instituted the Real Cédula de Gracias ("Royal Decree of Graces"), a law that afforded Spaniards in the colonies greater commercial freedom, created a change in tax code, and loosened immigration laws, encouraging new European settlers to establish themselves in the Americas. The act brought an influx of immigration both from Europe and from other Spanish colonies, which were in the process of finalizing their independence. By 1826, only Cuba and Puerto Rico remained under Spanish rule, and thus they became popular destinations for emigrating Europeans escaping famine and political and social upheaval.

THE GRITO DE LARES

In the nineteenth century, control of Puerto Rico was mostly in the hands of Spaniards, divided between *peninsulares* (Spaniards born in Spain, that is, the Iberian Peninsula) and criollos (literally "creoles," those of pure Spanish descent born in the Americas). Neither group was completely willing to sever its ties with Spain. However, there was one notable attempt at independence, known as the Grito de Lares ("Cry of Lares"), on September 23, 1868.

Organized by Ramón Emeterio Betances, the Grito de Lares mustered the revolutionary forces of the island, including Lola Rodríguez de Tió, Mariana Bracetti, Manuel Rojas, and Mathias Brugman. The revolution was easily subdued, and all the rebels captured. Nevertheless, it is considered to have led to the abolition of slavery in 1873, one of the causes for which Betances strongly advocated. Many of its participants are now considered Puerto Rican heroes, and Betances is fondly remembered as the "Father of the Nation" in Puerto Rico.

The decree had important consequences for the fabric of Puerto Rican society. Many of the Spanish immigrants who came to Puerto Rico developed strong ties to the island while also maintaining a deep connection with Spain. If they were geographically now Puerto Rican, they clung quite strongly to their Spanish ties and heritage. The growth of a Puerto Rican

This 1860 chromolithograph titled *Panorama de San Juan de Puerto-Rico* depicts a nineteenth-century scene in the city of San Juan, including colonial subjects, the city's buildings, and San Juan Bay in the distance.

national consciousness in the nineteenth century is therefore paradoxical, as scholar Wadda Ríos-Fonts claims in her 2007 article "The Patriot as Expatriate: Travel and National Identity in Nineteenth-Century Puerto Rico." While the nineteenth century saw the birth and growth of a strong national sentiment, a corresponding strong independence movement was never firmly established.

CHAPTER TWO

Early Puerto Rican Migration to the States

The first wave of Puerto Rican migration to the United States took place around the time of the Spanish-American War of 1898, which gave Cuba its independence and turned Puerto Rico into a territory of the United States. However, Puerto Rican immigrant communities did exist in the United States before this first large-scale migration. Throughout the nineteenth century, Puerto Rican migrants took root in many of the United States' port cities.

Perhaps the first Puerto Rican residents in the mainland states were members of the merchant class. As early as 1830, Puerto Rican merchants were settling on the eastern seaboard of the United States in such cities as New York, New Haven, Boston, and Philadelphia. From there, they developed trade with Puerto Ricans back on the island. There were two main trading products: sugar and tobacco. While the sugar trade saw the rise of a highly educated (and predominantly white) Puerto Rican merchant class in the United States, the tobacco trade was responsible for the rise in migration of Puerto Rican cigar makers (mostly of mixed race) into the centers of American cigar manufacturing, namely New York, New Orleans, Tampa, and Philadelphia.

FIGHTING FOR INDEPENDENCE FROM ABROAD

Tabaqueros, or cigar makers, formed cohesive communities in the United States and were highly involved in education and politics. Much of what is known of those early Puerto Rican immigrant communities comes from the book *Memoirs of Bernardo Vega: A Contribution to the History of the Puerto Rican Community in New York*. Bernardo Vega was a cigar maker, activist, and writer. His memoirs (published in 1977) documented his life in New York City throughout the first half of the twentieth century. By Vega's account, there were already around three thousand cigar factories in New York City by 1894, some of which were operated out of

A great deal of information about early Puerto Rican immigrant communities in New York can be gleaned from *Memoirs of Bernardo Vega*. Photographed here, Vega was a cigar maker whose account of immigrant life in early twentieth-century New York reveals the adjustments Puerto Rican immigrants made to integrate into their adopted city's cultural and political life.

VISA

UNITED STAT

the owners' home. Of those, about five hundred were owned by Spaniards or Latinos living in the United States, and of those five hundred, many were Cuban and Puerto Rican.

INSIDE NEW YORK'S CIGAR FACTORIES

Far from any stereotype of the uneducated immigrant worker, the Hispanic *tabaqueros* living and working in New York in the late nineteenth and early twentieth centuries were highly intellectually and politically engaged. Each cigar factory had assigned readers among its workers, who would read on the factory floor while others continued with their work. A wide variety of texts were read: newspaper articles that kept workers abreast of the political and social situation in the United States and their countries of origin; varied works of literature (from the Spanish Cervantes to the Russian Dostoyevsky to the French Victor Hugo); and even, as Bernardo Vega explains in his memoirs, political manifestos, which familiarized tobacco workers with diverse political ideologies. The readings were far from passive. Workers engaged in animated discussions through which they increased their knowledge about the world and heightened their class consciousness.

Hispanic workers were among the first to organize and join unions, such as the Cigars Makers' International Union (CMIU). As recounted in Vega's memoirs, Puerto Rican and Cuban cigar makers were not only involved in union organizing, they were also participants in the Cuban and Puerto Rican independence movements, with New York and Florida as their bases of operations. Each tobacco factory had a committee responsible for raising funds for the independence movements back home, which were ideologically united by Ramón Emeterio Betances's idea of an Antillean Confederation of Spanish-speaking Caribbean nations free from colonial and American control. Thus, even before the first proper wave of migration of Puerto Ricans to the United States, New York was an intellectual center of operations for the independence movements of Cuba and Puerto Rico.

New York, then, was the political and cultural center of Puerto Rican immigrants, where Puerto Rican–American identity and culture first developed while shaping and strengthening the independence movement back home. In New York, Puerto Rican independence was supported by members of the professional classes living there, led most notably by Ramón Emeterio Betances (who lived in New York from 1869 to 1870) and Julio J. Henna, leader of the Puerto Rican Section of the Cuban Revolutionary Party in New York. Multiple associations were created with Antillean independence as their mission, in New York and other American cities, including many women-only groups, such as the Hijas de la Libertad ("Daughters of Freedom"), Las

Puerto Rico's "Father of the Nation," Ramón Emeterio Betances, developed the concept of "Antilles for the Antillean." His phrasing was a direct response to US president James Monroe's doctrine of "America for the Americans," which decried European colonial efforts in the Western Hemisphere and allowed the United States to go unchecked in furthering its interests in Latin America.

Patriotas ("The Women Patriots"), and La Liga Antillana ("The Antillean League").

While Puerto Ricans in the United States were raising funds for and promoting the cause of independence back home, many intellectuals on the island were looking to remain linked with Spain and simply achieve a status of autonomy. In 1887, Puerto Rican author and politician Luis Muñoz Rivera helped found the Autonomist Party, which sought a high degree of autonomy for the island over local matters while still retaining Spanish colonial oversight. At first, Spain rebuffed the Autonomists and many were jailed. However, the fervor for independence grew both in Puerto Rico and Cuba, threatening US economic interests.

Fearing the loss of two of its few remaining colonies, in November 1897, Spain granted both Cuba and Puerto Rico the Autonomic Charter. Puerto Ricans for the first time had access to a form of self-government and their own parliament. While the Spanish Crown retained the right to appoint a governor of Puerto Rico, the Autonomic Charter created two legislative chambers, or houses, (the Administration Council and the House of Representatives), most of whom were to be elected by the local populations. For the first time, Puerto Rican–born individuals (predominantly criollos) had the ability to manage their own affairs on the island, both politically and financially. In the case of the Administration Council, members had to be born on the island or residents for at least four years. The charter therefore emphasized the dual identity of many elite Puerto Ricans: Spanish by tradition and economic ties, but Puerto Rican by birth and residence. In Cuba, the charter did little to quell the ongoing revolts and demands for complete independence.

THE SPANISH-AMERICAN WAR

It was in this climate that the USS *Maine* battleship was sent to protect US economic interests in revolution-ready Cuba. However, on February 15, 1898, the ship exploded in the harbor of Havana. The event, which remains unexplained to

The USS *Maine* is shown sailing in this 1897 photograph. Its unexplained explosion and sinking in Havana Harbor led to the start of the Spanish-American War.

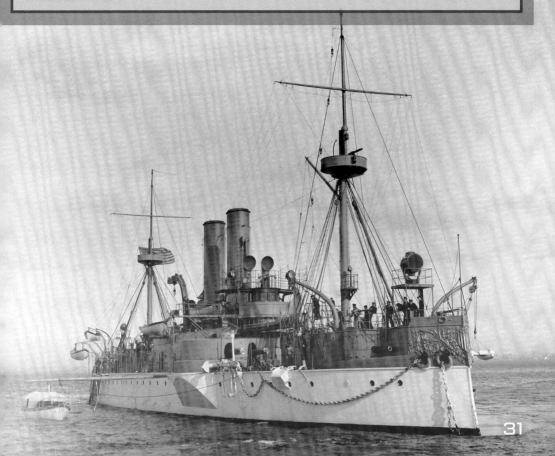

this day, created outrage among the American public, who assumed Spanish culpability for the explosion. The explosion of the USS *Maine* was the tipping point for a country already concerned with its financial interests, and it led to an American declaration of war on Spain on April 25, 1898.

In Puerto Rico, the conflict by land began on July 25, when General Nelson Miles and his infantrymen landed in Guánica. However, on August 13, 1898, not even four months after the conflict began, the Treaty of Paris was signed, ending the war between the United States and Spain. As per the terms of the treaty, the United States held temporary control of Cuba, which would become independent in 1902, and the territories of Puerto Rico, Guam, and the Philippines came under US control. While Spain had lost the last of its territories in America, the United States won preeminence as a powerful world military and political leader.

At the same time, the era marked a shift in the activities of Puerto Ricans and Cubans in the United States. The final meeting of the Puerto Rican section of the Cuban Revolutionary Party, as related by Bernardo Vega in his memoirs, was held on August 2, 1898. In his final speech in New York, Puerto Rican independence fighter Eugenio María de Hostos protested the unconditional annexation of Puerto Rico to the United States. Betances, then in Paris, warned: "I do not want us to be a colony, neither a colony of Spain nor a colony of the United States."

On the other hand, the Autonomist Muñoz Rivera traveled to the United States in an attempt at least to secure the same autonomy for Puerto Rico that he had managed to obtain from

Members of General Miles's army pose in this 1898 photograph before embarking for Puerto Rico during the Spanish-American War.

Spain. His efforts proved fruitless. Many on the island and in the United States accused him of facilitating and securing the transfer of the territory of Puerto Rico to the United States and considered him responsible for its continued colonial status.

An important chapter in Puerto Rican history had ended. An opportunity had been missed for Puerto Rico to obtain independence and become a sovereign state. However, in many ways, the conflict and its resolution led to the final consolidation of a Puerto Rican national identity that has continued with growing strength. It is a unique identity that encompasses both Puerto Ricans om the island and those living in the mainland United States.

Citizenship: A Double-Edged Sword

F rom the end of the Spanish-American War to the present, one of the main concerns that Puerto Ricans have had is their political status and relationship to the United States. This concern has been played out in the arena of citizenship and political participation in the affairs of the island and the mainland. Major General Joseph Wheeler's hopeful comments at the end of the war, which appear in the introduction to the photographic volume *Our Islands and*

Their People (1899), show just how fraught the beginning of the relationship between Puerto Rico and the United States was. Wheeler spoke of the United States' responsibility:

> *to lift [the people of Puerto Rico, Cuba, and the Philippines] from the low estate of unwilling subjects to the high plane of independent citizenship, to extend to them the knowledge of our beneficent institutions, and to help them onward and upward to the realization of the loftiest ideals of perfection in human government and the universal happiness of mankind.*

Such lofty ideals did not play out for Puerto Ricans, whose sovereignty remains, to this day, unrealized.

This 1899 political cartoon—shocking and appalling by today's standards—reflects the prevailing racist and imperialist attitudes of the time. The cartoon depicts Uncle Sam preparing to instruct four unruly students—the Philippines, Hawaii, "Porto Rico" (as many Americans insisted on spelling it at the time), and Cuba—while seemingly well-behaved "states" study quietly behind them.

FORAKER ACT

Although Wheeler spoke of an "independent citizenship," it is unclear exactly what form of citizenship he envisioned. Specifically for Puerto Rico, the aftermath of the war saw the imposition of military rule that lasted until the proclamation of the Foraker Act, signed into law by President McKinley on April 12, 1900. The Foraker Act instituted a civilian government and made a provision for Puerto Rican citizenship.

In *Experiencing Puerto Rican Citizenship and Cultural Nationalism*, scholar Jacqueline N. Font-Guzmán explains that the Foraker Act was a great disappointment to Puerto Ricans. The possibility of US citizenship, which some on the island did indeed desire, was debated at the time, though racist attitudes from members of Congress and their belief that Puerto Ricans had too distinct a cultural national identity led to the denial of US citizenship.

At the same time, the Foraker Act was written with the belief that Puerto Rico and its inhabitants were incapable of self-government. In line with that thinking, the act established that the governor, executive council, and other key government positions would be appointed directly by the United States. Additionally, in her text *Puerto Rican Diaspora*, Latino studies professor Carmen Teresa Whalen points out that the Foraker Act prohibited Puerto Rico from entering into negotiations with any other country or determining its own tariffs. It also required that all goods transported to Puerto Rico be shipped in US-owned vessels. This requisite became law in 1920 with the Merchant Marine Act.

Of course, because Puerto Ricans had enjoyed a measure of autonomy from Spain before the war began, the Foraker Act was seen as politically regressive. The forms of citizenship and government laid out by the Foraker Act gave Puerto Ricans neither the rights of a sovereign state nor a path to US citizenship and greater participation in the political affairs of the United States. Puerto Rican citizenship as defined by the Foraker Act could not be considered a real form of citizenship, for Puerto Rico was not recognized as an independent country. In spite of the proclamation, Puerto Rico continued to be nothing other than a US colony, and Puerto Ricans continued to be US subjects.

Another result of the transfer of power over Puerto Rico from Spain to the United States were new migratory patterns. The first Puerto Rican migration after the Spanish-American War entailed the recruitment of more than five thousand poor yet skilled Puerto Ricans laborers to Hawaii, a newly annexed US territory, where they were sent to work on the sugar plantations. The trip was long and gruesome: by sea to New Orleans, then train to California, and by sea again to Hawaii. Puerto Ricans faced serious racism that often developed into violence. In *Puerto Rican Diaspora*, Whalen notes that "by 1910, another 1,513 Puerto Ricans had settled in the continental United States, most of them in New York City." The situation was not to change much until the passage of a new act in 1917, which superseded the Foraker Act.

THE JONES-SHAFROTH ACT

By 1917, opinions in Washington had shifted regarding the Foraker Act. President Woodrow Wilson was in favor of extending citizenship to Puerto Ricans, and his fellow Democrats Representative William Atkinson Jones and Senator John F. Shafroth sponsored an act to accomplish just that. On March 2, 1917, the Jones-Shafroth Act was signed into law, granting all Puerto Ricans born since the beginning of the Spanish-American War US citizenship.

While it did reform some elements of Puerto Rico's system of government, important positions, including the governorship, were still to be appointed by the US government. The law allowed for Puerto Ricans to "opt out" of US citizenship and keep only their Puerto Rican citizenship; however, whoever

Senator John F. Shafroth of Colorado sponsored the Jones-Shafroth Act, which extended US citizenship to Puerto Ricans.

rescinded US citizenship could not participate legitimately in the political life of the island nor would their Puerto Rican citizenship be recognized internationally.

According to Font-Guzmán, many Puerto Rican politicians opposed US citizenship. Muñoz Rivera, then resident commissioner to the United States, was opposed to US citizenship because it would make it more difficult

PUERTO RICANS ARE US CITIZENS

The Jones-Shafroth Act , enacted in 1917, is the law that governs US citizenship for Puerto Ricans on the island. It is still in effect today. To some, it is the key that allows them to migrate at will from Puerto Rico to the mainland United States and back, and to enjoy some of the rights the United States gives its citizens. To others, the citizenship granted by the law was the imposition of a second-class citizenship that denies them the right to vote for president of the United States or full political participation in Congress. However one views it, the Jones-Shafroth Act sealed US citizenship for Puerto Ricans born on the island and made the migration patterns of Puerto Ricans quite distinct from any other migration into the United States.

VISA   UNITED STAT

for Puerto Ricans to gain independence, but others were opposed to it because it held no promise of a future transition to statehood. The Jones-Shafroth Act reasserted Puerto Rico's status as a territory of the United States. As economic historian James L. Dietz asserts in his text *Puerto Rico:*

Demonstrators in Chicago, Illinois, protest the United States' insufficient recovery efforts in Puerto Rico in the aftermath of Hurricane Maria. This protester's sign reads, "Free Puerto Rico! No to Colonization." Public opinion varies, but most polls show that a majority of Puerto Ricans are unhappy with the status quo.

Negotiating Development and Change, the act "guaranteed that political decisions would be governed by the interest of the United States, while US capital investments reoriented the economy." These economic changes had devastating effects on the Puerto Rican economy and produced an economy of dependence. As shall be seen, economics has been one of the most significant factors in the migratory patterns of Puerto Ricans to and from the mainland since the early twentieth century.

MYTHS AND FACTS

MYTH

All Puerto Ricans who have migrated to the mainland United States are uneducated and poor, and they've migrated only to benefit from the services available to them on the mainland.

FACT

Since the earliest days of Puerto Rican migration to the United States, Puerto Ricans were a diverse community composed of a highly educated merchant and intellectual class and a working class that sought to improve their education and knowledge. To this day, Puerto Rican migration is characterized by a mixture of socioeconomic and educational backgrounds.

MYTH

Puerto Ricans who have moved from Puerto Rico to the mainland United States, although citizens, are not allowed to vote in US elections.

FACT

Puerto Ricans who move to the mainland, establish their residency there, and register to vote can vote in all elections on the mainland, including presidential elections. As the Puerto Rican community on the mainland continues to grow, Puerto Ricans are in a position to make a real difference in US politics and forever change its landscape.

(continued on the next page)

(continued from the previous page)

MYTH

All Puerto Ricans want the territory to become the fifty-first state.

FACT

In three of five referendums on statehood, Puerto Ricans voted against becoming a state. In 2012, 61 percent of voters preferred statehood, though one-third of voters left that portion of their ballot blank in protest of the vote. A 2017 referendum yielded results that showed 97 percent of voters in favor of statehood, but voter turnout was historically low (just under 23 percent), causing few to take the results very seriously.

From Territory to Commonwealth

Migration patterns from Puerto Rico have generally followed, first and foremost, the economic conditions of the island, but not to be discounted are the effect of American views on Puerto Rico's resources, including its citizens. Among the effects of 1917's Jones-Shafroth Act was the removal of any remaining legal barriers to Puerto Rican entry to the United States.

PUERTO RICANS IN THE MILITARY

Within one month of the passage of the Jones-Shafroth Act, the United States entered World War I on the side of the Allies. During the course of the war, 236,000 Puerto Ricans registered to serve in the US armed forces and about 18,000 of them served, both in combat and in the United States in war industries

In this June 1951 photograph, members of the 65th Infantry Regiment sing during some downtime while serving in the Korean War. In April 2016, the regiment's members received a Congressional Gold Medal for their service.

and at military bases. The Puerto Rican division was eventually named the 65th Infantry Regiment, and the regiment went on to serve in World War II and the Korean War as well.

In the wake of World War I, the United States sought to limit immigration from war-torn Europe, though there continued to be a demand for cheap labor. Thus, Puerto Ricans were encouraged to move to the mainland United States. According to Whalen, in the period from about 1920 to 1940, the Puerto Rican population in the mainland United States grew from fewer than twelve thousand to nearly seventy

Puerto Rican teenagers hang out on a park bench in Spanish Harlem, New York City, in 1958. By the mid-twentieth century, New York City had become the center of Puerto Rican culture in the United States.

47

thousand, thanks in great part to the creation of contract labor programs. New York City had the largest Puerto Rican community on the mainland, and Puerto Ricans settled mostly on the Lower East Side (often referred to in Spanglish as Loisaida) as well as in El Barrio (or Spanish Harlem). Other sizable Puerto Rican communities were established in Philadelphia, Boston, Connecticut, Chicago, and San Francisco.

SQUASHING THE NATIONALIST PARTY

Though Puerto Rico's status as a US territory did provide its people the benefits of unhindered migration that US citizenship provided, discontent with a poorly disguised colonial arrangement continued to exist on the island. Throughout the 1940s, Puerto Rico's Nationalist Party promoted the cause of independence, though the US-friendly Popular Democratic Party (PPD) had greater success in elections. The passage of Law 53 of 1948, which criminalized public displays in support of independence, sought to squash the Nationalist Party's activities. In turn, the PPD continued to dominate politics on the island.

In 1947, Congress passed the Elective Governors Act, which allowed Puerto Rico to elect a governor for the first time. In 1948, the PPD's leader Luis Muñoz Marín became the first democratically elected governor of Puerto Rico. Muñoz Marín served as governor from 1949 until 1965. On July 3, 1950, the Puerto Rico Federal Relations Act was signed into law,

On June 10, 1948, the last US-appointed governor of Puerto Rico and member of the PPD, Jesús T. Piñeiro, signed into law an act known as Law 53. Referred to as the Ley de la Mordaza ("Gag Law"), the law made it a criminal offense to pursue any activity that could be seen as having the intent of overthrowing the established government of Puerto Rico or of impeding its activities. As a result of the law, public displays in support of Puerto Rican independence, such as singing the Puerto Rican anthem and carrying the Puerto Rican flag, became punishable acts. The law targeted individuals who supported independence, chief among them Pedro Albizu Campos, leader of the Nationalist Party. As Puerto Rican history professor Ivonne Acosta explains in her work on the act, *La Mordaza: Puerto Rico 1948–1957*, the measure was passed just before Puerto Ricans were allowed for the first time to elect their own governor, and it was intended to reduce the growth of the independence movement and clear the way for the constitution of 1952, which reaffirmed Puerto Rico's relationship to the United States.

allowing Puerto Ricans to organize their own local government and laws and to draft their own constitution. However, all legal changes were to be done under the strict supervision and approval of the US president and Congress. That same year, on

Following the attempted assassination of President Truman, Nationalist Party leader Pedro Albizu Campos was arrested on November 2, 1950, in San Juan. Albizu Campos is the subject wearing suspenders, flanked on either side by the arresting officers.

November 1, two members of the Nationalist Party failed at an assassination attempt against US president Harry S. Truman. The attempt brought renewed US attention to the political limbo of Puerto Rico, and Truman lent his support to a constitutional referendum.

BECOMING A COMMONWEALTH

On March 3, 1952, the constitutional referendum was held and lacking an option to support outright independence, about 82 percent of Puerto Ricans voted in favor of a new constitution and the end of Puerto Rico's territorial status. On July 25, 1952, the Puerto Rican Constitution came into effect, and Puerto Rico became what is known in Spanish as an *estado libre asociado* (ELA, literally "free associated state"). That political formula remains in effect to this day.

Significantly, the English translation of *estado libre asociado* is most commonly given as "commonwealth," and the constitution makes clear that Puerto Rico is an unincorporated territory of the United States. However, as Font-Guzmán argues in *Experiencing Puerto Rican Citizenship*, the term in Spanish holds a strong symbolic meaning: it was meant to be "free" to appease those who sought independence from the United States, "associated" for those who wanted some kind of annexation with autonomy, and a "state" for those whose ultimate goal was to become a US state.

In terms of citizenship, the ratification of a new constitution and birth of the "commonwealth" did not create any real changes from the rights Puerto Ricans were ceded in the Jones-

Governor Luiz Muñoz Marín stands with US president John F. Kennedy in this 1961 photograph. As governor, Muñoz Marín oversaw Puerto Rico's transition from US territory to a commonwealth in the 1950s.

Shafroth Act. While citizens, Puerto Ricans on the island still could not participate in US national politics, and they gained no voting representation in Congress or the possibility of voting for president. At the same time, federal legislation could still overrule Puerto Rican laws, and no change of government or relationship between the island and the United States, or for that matter any other country in the world, would happen without US approval.

The Situation Today

The political formula of the estado libre asociado came with a swift transition for Puerto Rico from an agrarian economy to an industrialized one, spurred on by an investment program known as Operación Manos a la Obra ("Operation Bootstrap"). Historian James L. Dietz called this program "industrialization by invitation." It provided incentives to attract US investors to the island and promote industrialization by providing cheaper labor than on the mainland, foregoing taxes, and importing raw materials in order to export finished products.

During this period, Dietz explains, Puerto Rico entered new industries, including pharmaceuticals, machinery, and electronics, while allowing its agricultural economy and the food, tobacco, and clothing industries to collapse. To assist in the process of industrialization, the Puerto Rican legislature established the Bureau of Employment and Migration within the Department of Labor in 1947, intended to increase the rate of migration to the mainland of the Puerto Rican workforce displaced from their jobs in agriculture and other industries. The bureau was also established to ensure that the migration would move beyond New York and into other cities across the nation.

NEW WAVES OF MIGRATION

By 1970, the United States was home to 810,000 Puerto Rican migrants and an additional 581,000 mainland-born Puerto Ricans. Of those, 59 percent lived in New York, while other communities formed in the Midwest, New England, and the Mid-Atlantic. According to Whalen, the decades between 1970 and 2000 saw much two-way migration, with many laborers returning to the island as they saw themselves displaced from cities across the mainland, where the increase of technical jobs left migrant workers with few opportunities. However, more islanders left for the mainland than went back to resettle, mostly due to an economy of dependence, a decrease in jobs on the island, and the establishment of a minimum wage, which made Puerto

In this 1970 photograph, a street vendor sells flowers, toy cars, and other goods on a sidewalk in El Barrio. At that time, 59 percent of Puerto Ricans living on the mainland were concentrated in New York City.

Rico a less desirable location than other Caribbean countries for US investors. Ultimately, this period saw continuous migration between the mainland and the island, as workers tried and failed to secure positions in either of the two unwelcoming economies.

During the 1980s and '90s, migration to the US mainland increased, and the pool of migrants started to contain a large number of professionals, many of whom had gone to school on the mainland. In the 1980s, the destinations of these migrants were concentrated mostly in Florida, although some Puerto Ricans also moved to California and Texas.

By the 2000 US census, Puerto Rico had become a divided nation; equal numbers of Puerto Ricans lived in the mainland United States (3,623,392) and in Puerto Rico (3,406,178). A Pew Center statistical research study published in 2010 revealed that 4.7 million Americans in the United States identify as Puerto Rican, compared to the 3.7 million living on the island that same year. Of those mainland Puerto Ricans, 52 percent lived in the Northeast, with 23 percent in New York City alone. Twenty percent lived in the South, with 18 percent of them in Florida. Of course, following 2017's devastating Hurricane Maria, those numbers have changed drastically, and the mainland is seeing a boom in migration of Puerto Ricans of all ages, social classes, and levels of education.

A COMMUNITY DIVIDED

Despite the uniquely bidirectional migration patterns of Puerto Ricans, political ideologies of Puerto Ricans on the mainland and those on the island have not always run parallel to each other. Even culturally, Puerto Ricans on the island have not always looked at Puerto Ricans on the mainland as full-fledged Puerto Ricans. In many ways, divisions have been produced by discrimination based on race, social class, and language (many Puerto Ricans on the mainland speak Spanglish, which many island Puerto Ricans view with derision).

In the late 1960s and 1970s, so-called Nuyoricans focused on their experiences with racism and other sociopolitical issues in their community. From the Nuyorican Poets, who founded the Nuyorican Poets Cafe on the Lower East Side in 1973, to

Posters in San Juan encourage voters to choose statehood ahead of the June 2017 referendum on Puerto Rico's political status. While 97 percent of voters chose statehood, voter turnout was at a historic low of 23 percent, causing few to take the results seriously.

the founders of El Museo del Barrio (an art museum dedicated to Latino arts) and the radical Young Lords group of leftist activists, Puerto Ricans in New York were proudly supporting the cause of Puerto Rican independence. Meanwhile, in 1968, Puerto Ricans on the island elected a governor from the New Progressive Party, whose platform centers around achieving statehood for Puerto Rico.

In truth, just as Puerto Ricans have moved continuously between Puerto Rico and the mainland United States, so too have the three ideologies of independence, annexation with autonomy, and statehood moved into higher or lesser prominence on the island and the mainland. Today, three main parties dominate politics on the island, with platforms determined by their members' desired relationship with the United States. The New Progressive Party (PNP) has, since its inception in 1967, worked for Puerto Rico to become the fifty-first state of the United States. The Independence Party (PIP) has consistently pursued independence. Finally, the Popular Democratic Party (PPD) would like to maintain the island's status as a commonwealth.

HOW CAN PUERTO RICO BECOME A STATE?

The US Constitution establishes the guidelines for admission of new states to the Union. Article IV, Section 3, Clause 1 of the Constitution reads:

New States may be admitted by the Congress into this Union; but no new State shall be formed or erected within the Jurisdiction of any other State; nor any State be formed by the Junction of two or more States, or Parts of States, without the Consent of the Legislatures of the States concerned as well as of the Congress.

As such, new states can only be brought into being by Congress.

Historically, new states are most often formed from existing territories whose population, through a referendum, expressed a desire for statehood. Upon ratifying a state constitution, Congress has then voted to admit the new state.

While referendums on statehood have showed Puerto Ricans in favor of becoming a state, they have suffered from low voter turnout. Partisan politics in Washington also present an obstacle to Puerto Rican statehood, as one political party will likely benefit from additional voting representation. While Puerto Rico is certainly eligible to become a state, it is unlikely to be admitted to the union in the near future.

This ideological friction has played out in the National Puerto Rican Day Parade in New York. Founded in 1958, the parade is the largest-scale display of Puerto Rican pride and unity in the United States. The organizers of the parade in 2000 decided to dedicate it to Pedro Albizu Campos. The decision provoked the anger of the prostatehood Puerto Ricans on the island, who saw Albizu Campos as a symbol of terrorism— not national pride. A fiercer controversy arose in 2017, when the parade decided to honor Oscar López Rivera, a member of the proindependence Armed Forces of National Liberation, responsible for a bombing campaign throughout the 1970s and '80s in New York and other American cities. In protest, many corporations backed out of sponsoring the event.

A divisive figure among Puerto Ricans, Oscar López Rivera was convicted on conspiracy charges for his organization's bombing campaign that lasted from 1974 until 1983. In 1999, President Bill Clinton pardoned López Rivera along with sixteen other members of the Armed Forces of National Liberation.

Yet, despite cultural and political differences, there is far more that unites than separates Puerto Ricans everywhere. From the salsa sounds of Tito Puente to the jazz grooves of Miguel Zenón; from the baseball stardom of Roberto Clemente and Carlos Beltrán to the writings of Ana Lydia Vega, Julia de Burgos, and Lourdes Vázquez, the cultural production of Puerto Ricans everywhere is shared by all and energized by the continuous movement between the island and the mainland. And, as the response to Hurricane Maria has shown, the Puerto Rican national identity remains powerful, and the bonds among all Puerto Ricans continue to grow stronger.

VISA   UNITED STATES

AN UNCERTAIN FUTURE

On November 27, 2017, Altagracia del Valle returned to San Juan, Puerto Rico, after water, electricity, and phone service in her home had been partially restored. She was one of the lucky ones, since as of January 2018, one-third of the island remained without power as the US Federal Emergency Management Agency prepared to end its deliveries of food and clean drinking water. Since then, del Valle's children, grandchildren, and other relatives in the mainland United States have visited her, and some have considered relocating back to the island. Far from any stereotype of migrant communities, her family includes professors, computer programmers, photographers, flight attendants, physical therapists, activists, dancers, veterinarians, contractors, architects, and many more, living in Puerto Rico and on the mainland. Her case is most certainly not unique.

Many Puerto Ricans in the United States will continue to visit the island and maintain a strong sense of national pride and identity. Some will stay. Many on the island have and will continue to come to the mainland. They may or may not return to the island. Unless the relationship between Puerto Rico and the United States changes, Puerto Ricans as a group will remain in constant motion, coming and going freely between the Caribbean island and the mainland United States.

PUERTO RICANS IN THE MAINLAND UNITED STATES

Population on the mainland
4,623,716

States with the largest Puerto Rican communities
New York: 1,070,558
Florida: 847,550
New Jersey: 434,092
Pennsylvania: 366,082
Massachusetts: 266,125

Cities with the largest Puerto Rican communities
New York City: 723,621
Philadelphia: 121,643
Chicago: 102,703

Notable mainland-born Puerto Rican entertainers

Marc Anthony	Tito Puente
Willie Colón	Richie Ray
Jennifer Lopez	Chita Rivera
Lin-Manuel Miranda	Bobby Sanabria
Charlie Palmieri	
Rosie Perez	

VISA   UNITED STAT

Notable mainland-based Puerto Rican writers and artists

Jean-Michel Basquiat
Pure Belpré
Jesús Colón
Nelson Antonio Denis
Sandra María Esteves
Victor Hernández Cruz
Tato Laviera
Nicholasa Mohr
Raphael Montañez Ortiz

Pedro Pietri
Miguel Piñero
Manuel Rivera-Ortiz
Esmeralda Santiago
Piri Thomas
Edwin Torres
Lourdes Vázquez
Ed Vega
William Carlos Williams

Notable mainland-based Puerto Rican athletes

Roberto Alomar
José Juan Barea
Wilfred Benítez
Roberto Clemente
Butch Lee

Sidney Rivera
Chi-Chi Rodríguez
Daniel Santiago
Bernie Williams

Notable mainland-born Puerto Ricans in US politics

Sonia Sotomayor (associate justice of the Supreme Court)
Maurice Ferré (former mayor of Miami)
Herman Badillo (US representative from New York)

1493 Christopher Columbus discovers the island of Borikén during his second voyage.

1509 Juan Ponce de León becomes the first governor of Puerto Rico.

1815 The Real Cédula de Gracias is instituted, giving Spaniards in the colonies greater economic freedom and reforming immigration laws.

1826 Following the Latin American wars of independence, Cuba and Puerto Rico are the only remaining Spanish colonies in the Americas.

1868 The independence rebellion known as the Grito de Lares ("Cry of Lares") is stopped by the Spaniards.

1873 In response to the Grito de Lares, slavery is abolished in the Spanish colonies.

1887 Luis Muñoz Rivera helps found the Autonomist Party.

1897 Spain grants the Autonomic Charter, giving Puerto Ricans greater financial and political freedom.

1898 The Spanish-American War occurs, as a result of which Puerto Rico becomes a territory of the United States following the signing of the Treaty of Paris.

1900 The Foraker Act institutes a civilian government in Puerto Rico fully controlled by the United States.

1917 The Jones-Shafroth Act is signed into law, granting Puerto Ricans US citizenship.

1920 The Merchant Marine Act makes it mandatory that all commercial vessels entering the ports of Puerto Rico must be US-owned vessels.

VISA

1948 Law 53 is passed, prohibiting public displays of Puerto Rican nationalism. Luis Muñoz Marín becomes the first governor of Puerto Rico elected by popular vote.

1950 Puerto Rican nationalists attempt to assassinate Harry S. Truman.

1952 A new Puerto Rican constitution comes into effect, turning the territory into an estado libre asociado, or commonwealth, of the United States.

1958 New York's National Puerto Rican Day Parade first occurs.

1967 The New Progressive Party is founded with the aim of achieving statehood for Puerto Rico.

1969 The Museo del Barrio is founded in East Harlem.

1970 The United States is home to 810,000 Puerto Rican migrants and an additional 581,000 mainland-born Puerto Ricans.

1973 The Nuyorican Poets Cafe is founded on the Lower East Side of Manhattan.

2000 Roughly equal numbers of Puerto Ricans live on the island and in the mainland United States.

2017 Hurricane Maria hits the island of Puerto Rico, causing extensive damage and driving a new wave of migration to the mainland.

abolition The ending of slavery.

advocate To defend a cause or proposal.

Antilles The islands of the Caribbean Sea, excluding the Bahamas.

appoint To name someone to a specific position.

autonomy The quality of having some form of self-government.

bidirectional Describing movement in two opposite directions.

citizenship A member of a country with the rights and privileges established by it.

colony A territory that has economic ties and is politically subservient to a parent state.

conquest The act of winning over a territory or a people through war or force.

constitution Principles and laws of a nation that establish its rights and form of government.

criollo A Spaniard born in the Americas.

derision A feeling of contempt generally expressed through ridicule or scorn.

diaspora The movement or migration of an ethnic group of people from their traditional homeland elsewhere.

discrimination The act of treating a person or group of people worse than another, depriving that group or person of equality.

encomienda A system by which colonial land and its indigenous inhabitants were given to Spanish colonists for economic purposes.

heritage Tradition or legacy acquired from one's ancestors.

infrastructure The basic foundation or framework of a system.

manifesto A written declaration of the beliefs of a movement or ideology.

migration Movement from one place to another.

referendum A vote held on a measure proposed or passed by a legislature or a popular initiative.

Santeria A religion practiced predominantly in Cuba that combines indigenous African Yoruba faith with elements of Roman Catholicism and its saints.

sovereign Having full control of one's own political powers or authority.

Spanglish A form of Spanish that borrows heavily from English.

supersede To replace or override something previously established.

syncretic Characterized by a fusion of different elements or ideas.

Taino A member of the indigenous Arawakan people.

tariff Duties that must be paid to the government on imported goods.

union An association of workers that advocates collectively for their rights, working conditions, and pay.

Center for Puerto Rican Studies (Centro)
Hunter College
695 Park Avenue, Room E1429
New York, NY 10065
(212) 772-4197
Website: https://centropr.hunter.cuny.edu
Facebook: @centropr
Twitter: @centroPR
YouTube: @CentroPR
The Center for Puerto Rican Studies is a research institute at
    Hunter College dedicated to studying the Puerto Rican
    experience in the United States. It has a vast archive of
    historical and cultural information about island and
    mainland Puerto Ricans.

El Museo del Barrio
1230 5th Avenue
New York, NY 10029
(212) 831-7272
Website: http://www.elmuseo.org
Facebook, Twitter, and Instagram: @elmuseo
YouTube: @ElMuseodelBarrioNY
El Museo del Barrio preserves and presents the arts of Latino,
    Caribbean, and Latin American cultures, including Puerto
    Rico. It hosts celebrations and educational programs on
    Latino arts and cultures.

National Museum of Puerto Rican Arts & Culture
    (NMPRAC)
3015 West Division Street
Chicago, IL 60622
(773) 486-8345
Website: http://nmprac.org
Facebook: @nmprac
Twitter: @mynmprac
The NMPRAC is the premier organization dedicated to
    the promotion and celebration of Puerto Rican arts and
    culture in the United States.

National Puerto Rican Day Parade (NPRDP)
PO Box 975
New York, NY 10272
Website: https://www.nprdpinc.org
Facebook: @NationalPuertoRicanParade
Twitter and Instagram: @prparadenyc
The annual NPRDP is the largest celebration of cultural pride
    in the United States. It revels in the accomplishments
    and contributions of the more than five million Puerto
    Ricans living on the mainland. In addition to the parade,
    the organization promotes Puerto Rican arts, culture, and
    education and provides scholarships to students of Puerto
    Rican descent.

Puerto Rican Arts Alliance (PRAA)
3000 North Elbridge Avenue
Chicago, IL 60618
(773) 342-8865
Website: www.praachicago.org
Facebook: @PuertoRicanArtsAlliance
Twitter: @PRAACHICAGO
YouTube: @PuertoricanAA
The PRAA preserves and promotes Puerto Rican art through
    events and art education programs, collaborating with
    community centers and public schools in the Chicago area.

Puerto Rican Arts Diaspora of Orlando (PRADO)
12427 South Orange Blossom Trail
Orlando, FL 32837
(407) 925-2910
Website: https://www.ladiasporapr.com
Facebook: @ladiasporapr
The Mission of the Puerto Rican Arts Diaspora of Orlando
    is to maintain and educate people about the work
    of Puerto Rican artists and to promote awareness of
    Hispanic culture.

Schomburg Center for Research in Black Culture
515 Malcolm X Boulevard
New York, NY 10037
(917) 275-6975
Website: https://www.nypl.org/locations/schomburg
A branch of the New York Public Library, the Schomburg

Center for Research in Black Culture houses the personal archives of Arturo Schomburg, a Puerto Rican activist, historian, and writer of African descent. Among other documents, the center holds documents on slavery and African culture in Puerto Rico.

Sociedad Herencia Puertorriqueña/Puerto Rican Heritage
    Society (SHP)
PO Box 460206
San Antonio, TX 78246
Website: http://www.sociedadherenciaprsa.org
Facebook: @CoquiSA.org
Founded in 1984, the SHP is devoted to the promotion
    and advancement of Puerto Rican culture through
    annual festivals and other cultural events. In addition to
    participating in diverse charitable causes, the SHP grants
    four to six scholarships each year to graduating high
    school seniors.

FOR FURTHER READING

Barrington, Richard. *Sonia Sotomayor: The Supreme Court's First Hispanic Justice* (Making a Difference: Leaders Who Are Changing the World). New York, NY: Britannica Educational Publishing, 2015.

Bjorklund, Ruth, and Richard Hantula. *Puerto Rico: The Island of Enchantment* (It's My State). New York, NY: Cavendish Square Publishing, 2016.

Boehme, Gerry. *Roberto Clemente: The Pride of Puerto Rico* (Game-Changing Athletes). New York, NY: Cavendish Square Publishing, 2016.

Clinton, Greg. *Puerto Rico and the Spanish-American War* (Expanding America). New York, NY: Cavendish Square Publishing, 2016.

Duany, Jorge. *Puerto Rico: What Everyone Needs to Know.* New York, NY: Oxford University Press, 2017.

Harrison, Kathryn. *Lin-Manuel Miranda: Composer, Actor, and Creator of* Hamilton (Influential Lives). New York, NY: Enslow Publishing, 2018.

Johanson, Paula, and Robert Somerlott. *The Spanish-American War* (United States at War). New York, NY: Enslow Publishing, 2017.

Niver, Heather Moore. *Juan Ponce de León: First Explorer of Florida and First Governor of Puerto Rico* (Spotlight on Explorers and Colonization). New York, NY: Rosen Publishing, 2017.

Torres, John. *Sonia Sotomayor: First Latina Supreme Court Justice* (Influential Latinos). New York, NY: Enslow Publishing, 2016.

Toth, Henrietta. *Christopher Columbus: Explorer and Colonizer of the New World* (Spotlight on Explorers and Colonization). New York, NY: Rosen Publishing, 2017.

Worth, Richard. *Puerto Rico: From Colony to Commonwealth* (Our Shared History). New York, NY: Enslow Publishing, 2016.

Acosta, Ivonne. *La Mordaza: Puerto Rico, 1948-1957*. Río Piedras, PR: Editorial Edil, 2008.

Acosta Cruz, María. *Dream Nation: Puerto Rican Culture and the Fictions of Independence*. New Brunswick, NJ: Rutgers University Press, 2014.

Carrión, María Elena. "Real Cédula de Gracia (1815)." Enciclopedia de Puerto Rico. Retrieved February 27, 2018. https://enciclopediapr.org/en/encyclopedia/real -cedula-de-gracia-1815.

Cruz, Zahira. "The Autonomic Charter of 1897." Enciclopedia de Puerto Rico. September 12, 2014. https://enciclopediapr.org/en/encyclopedia/the -autonomic-charter-of-1897.

Dietz, James L. *Puerto Rico: Negotiating Development and Change*. Boulder, CO: Lynne Rienner, 2003.

Font-Guzmán, Jacqueline. *Experiencing Puerto Rican Citizenship and Cultural Nationalism*. New York, NY: Palgrave Macmillan, 2015.

Hendrickson, Kenneth E. *The Spanish-American War*. Westport, CT: Greenwood Press, 2003.

González, José Luis. *Puerto Rico: The Four-Storeyed Country and Other Essays*. Princeton, NJ: Markus Wiener Publishers, 2013.

Martínez-Cruzado, JC, et al. "Reconstructing the population history of Puerto Rico by means of mtDNA phylogeographic analysis." *American Journal of Physical Anthropology*. Vol. 128. Sept. 2005. 131–155.

Monge, José Trías. *Puerto Rico: The Trials of the Oldest Colony in the World*. New Haven, CT: Yale University

Press, 1997.

Motel, Seth, and Eileen Patten. "Hispanics of Puerto Rican Origin in the United States, 2010. Statistical Profile." Pew Research Center. June 27, 2012. http://www.pewhispanic .org/2012/06/27/hispanics-of-puerto-rican-origin-in-the -united-states-2010.

Olivares, José de, William S. Bryan, and Joseph Wheeler. *Our Islands and Their People as Seen with Camera and Pencil.* New York, NY: N. D. Thompson Publishing Co., 1899.

Otfinoski, Steven. *Juan Ponce de León: Discoverer of Florida.* New York, NY: Benchmark Books, 2005.

Pérez y González, María E. *Puerto Ricans in the United States* (The New Americans). Westport, CT: Greenwood Press, 2000.

Ramos-Zayas, Ana Y. *National Performances. The Politics of Class, Race, and Space in Puerto Rican Chicago.* Chicago, IL: University of Chicago Press, 2003.

Rhianon, Alexis. "All the Guests on Lin-Manuel Miranda's 'Almost Like Praying' That Joined Forces to Support Puerto Rico." *Bustle*, October 6, 2017. https://www .bustle.com/p/all-the-guests-on-lin-manuel-mirandas -almost-like-praying-that-joined-forces-to-support -puerto-rico-2802006.

Rodríguez Vecchini, Hugo. "Foreword: Back and Forward." *The Commuter Nation: Perspectives on Puerto Rican Migration.* Torre, Carlos Antonio, Hugo Rodríguez Vecchini, and Williams Burgos, ed. Río Piedras, PR: Editorial de la Universidad de Puerto Rico, 1994.

Sesin, Carmen. "Over 200,000 Puerto Ricans Have Arrived in Florida Since Hurricane Maria." NBC News, November 30, 2017. https://www.nbcnews.com/news/latino/over -200-000-puerto-ricans-have-arrived-florida-hurricane -maria-n825111.

Tapia y Rivera, Alejandro. *Mis memorias: o, Puerto Rico como lo encontré y como lo dejo*. Río Piedras, PR: Editorial Edil, 1996.

Torre, Carlos Antonio, ed. *The Commuter Nation: Perspectives on Puerto Rican Migration*. Río Piedras, PR: Editorial de la Universidad de Puerto Rico, 1994.

Vega, Bernardo. *Memoirs of Bernardo Vega: A Contribution to the History of the Puerto Rican Community in New York*. New York, NY: Monthly Review Press, 1984.

Whalen, Carmen Teresa. *Puerto Rican Diaspora: Historical Perspectives*. Philadelphia, PA: Temple University Press, 2008.

Wilson, Michael. "A Subdued Puerto Rican Parade Marches On." *New York Times*, June 11, 2017. https://www .nytimes.com/2017/06/11/nyregion/puerto-rican-day -parade.html.

INDEX

VISA UNITED STAT

ABOUT THE AUTHOR

Lourdes Dávila was born in Puerto Rico. She is an associate clinical professor at New York University, where she teaches Latin American and Caribbean literature and culture, writes and publishes about the relationship of photography and movement with literature, and manages the journal *Esferas*. She was a professional dancer in Puerto Rico and in New York. She lives in New York with her husband, Peter Stewart, her daughter, Beatriz Juana, and their dog, Benny.

PHOTO CREDITS

Cover, p. 3 lev radin/Shutterstock.com; pp. 6–7 The Washington Post /Getty Images; pp. 11, 50 Bettmann/Getty Images; pp. 15, 20 DEA/G. Dagli Orti/De Agostini/Getty Images; p. 16 Universal Images Group /Getty Images; p. 18 Rhona Wise/AFP/Getty Images; p. 23 The New York Public Library Digital Collections; p. 26 Walter Oleksy /Alamy Stock Photo; p. 29 Paul Fearn/Alamy Stock Photo; pp. 31, 39 Library of Congress Prints and Photographs Division; p. 33 Hulton Archive/Archive Photos/Getty Images; p. 36 Universal History Archive /Universal Images Group/Getty Images; p. 41 Anadolu Agency /Getty Images; p. 46 © AP Images; p. 47 Stan Wayman/The LIFE Picture Collection/Getty Images; p. 52 Paul Schutzer/The LIFE Picture Collection /Getty Images; p. 55 ullstein bild/Getty Images; p. 57 AFP /Getty Images; p. 60 Nima Taradji/Polaris/Newscom; interior pages designs (portrait collage) Ollyy/Shutterstock.com, (USA stamp) ducu59us /Shutterstock.com, (fingerprint) Rigamondis/Shutterstock.com, (brochure) Konstanin L/Shutterstock.com, (visa) Sergiy Palamarchuk /Shutterstock.com.

Design: Nelson Sá; Layout: Nicole Russo-Duca; Editor: Jacob R. Steinberg; Photo Researcher: Bruce Donnola